# Salamander Rain

## A Lake & Pond Journal

Written and Illustrated
by Kristin Joy Pratt-Serafini

# Lakes & Ponds

This is Mr. Green. He is my favorite frog in our pond.

ME

KORi

Spider Lake

Grandma's house

miles

kilometers

## The Lake & Pond Report
by Melvin Waterpepper,
Leader of Wetland Patrol No. 1

### WATER, WATER EVERYWHERE!

Did you know that there are approximately 100,000 lakes (each bigger than 100 acres) in the United States and even more in Canada? That's a lot of water! That doesn't count all the smaller lakes and ponds. Even so, all the lakes and ponds in the entire world make up only a tiny part of Earth's water. In fact, if all the water on Earth is equal to one dollar, then all the water in all the world's lakes and ponds would equal less than a penny! The great majority of water on this planet is salty ocean water.

### HOW LAKES AND PONDS WERE FORMED:

Lakes and ponds can be formed in many different ways. In Canada and the Northern United States, they were carved out by glaciers. In the Southeast, lake basins were formed by ancient receding oceans. In the West, there are glacial lakes high up in the mountains, and desert lakes that form in sandy depressions when the water table rises. Some extinct volcano craters even turn into lakes.

### WHY ARE LAKES AND PONDS SO IMPORTANT?

Lakes and ponds are very important to humans, and other animals and plants too. They provide us with water for drinking and irrigation. Many lakes also make great vacation spots. Ducks, frogs, beavers, trout and many other animals need lakes and ponds for nesting, breeding, eating and hiding from predators. There are so many creatures living in lakes, ponds, and other wetlands ecosystems that wetlands have almost as much biodiversity as tropical rainforests!

### WHO CAN HELP?

It is not someone else's job to clean up and protect our lakes and ponds. We each have the capacity and the responsibility to take action ourselves. Go Wetland Patrol!

## Official Planet Scout Journal

### by Klint

28 February

Dear Journal,

This starts my third year as a Planet Scout! My older sister, Kori, is also a Planet Scout. We love to explore together outside. The more I tromp through forests and get muddy in ponds, the more I'm in awe of these amazing places and the animals that live there! Exploring the neighborhood pond is so fun that Kori and I joined the Wetland Patrol of the Planet Scouts. Wetland Patrol members study and protect freshwater wetlands. Each member is working to become an expert on one wetland habitat. There are four kinds of wetlands that we can study: marshes and swamps, bogs and fens, lakes and ponds, and rivers and streams. They are all very wet! Of course Kori and I volunteered to study lakes and ponds. This journal is where I will gather all my information about them this year.

# Our Neighbor-hood Pond.

Red Maple Tree

Blue Flag

Lawn

Cattails

Rocks

Turtle Log

Woods

yards

meters

# Planet Scout Stuff:

journal

boots

shovel

pencil

binoculars

camera

bucket

from the Wetland Watchers Magazine

# How Lakes & Ponds Are Different:

What makes a lake a lake and a pond a pond? Generally, ponds are smaller and shallower than lakes. A pond is shallow enough to have water plants like water milfoil or waterlilies growing all over the bottom, while a lake is too deep in the middle to support plants. The main difference is temperature, though. Ponds are small enough to maintain the same temperature all the way to the bottom. On a warm day, the whole pond is warm. A lake, however, has layers. In the summer, the top layer can be as much as 30 degrees warmer than the bottom. But in the winter, the top of a lake can freeze into solid ice, while the bottom remains just warm enough to stay liquid.

RED SALAMANDER

pseudotriton ruber

TWO-LINED SALAMANDER

eur bisLi

MUD SALAMANDER

pseudotriton montans

TIGER SALAMANDER

ambystoma tigrinum

EASTERN NEWT

March 10

I just finished my math homework, listening to the rain on the window, when Kori came into my room with two flashlights and said it was time for a night hike! She said the first warm rain of the year had just started. I know what that means! Salamander Rain! On the night of the first warm rain of the year, Spotted Salamanders migrate to pools and ponds, where they raise their babies. We headed to a pool in the valley below our neighbor's house.

Kori was right! There were salamanders everywhere, scrambling over twigs, rocks and each other to get to the water. Where were they all hiding? We had to walk slowly and carefully to avoid stepping on any. This was our first serious wetland exploration, and we got seriously wet!

cea
ata

taricha
torsa

CALIFORNIA
NEWT

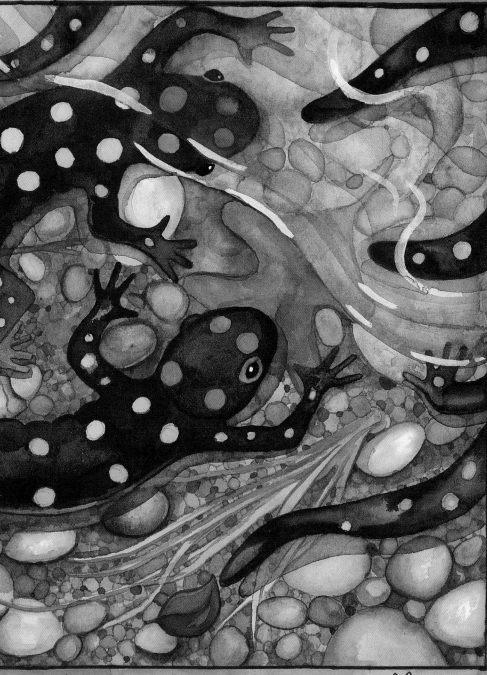

eurycea
quadridigitata

ndophthalmus DWARF
meridionalis SALAMANDER

BLACK-
SPOTTED
NEWT

notophthalmus
viridescens

PACIFIC
GIANT
SALAMANDER

dicamptodon
ensatus

# SPOTTED SALAMANDER
## (Ambystoma maculatum)

LENGTH: 6-9.75" (15.2-24.8 cm)
HABITAT: hardwood forests and hillsides around pools and flooded swampy depressions

## A Salamander's Life Cycle

*by Gretchen Askers*

Spotted Salamanders live in the forest during most of the year. They hide in vacant mammal burrows and under leaf litter on the forest floor. Because adult Spotted Salamanders spend most of their time underground, they are rarely seen in the forest.

"In the early spring, they are motivated by heavy rains and warming temperatures to migrate to vernal pools," explains Phyllis Slitherton, a volunteer at the Twin Oaks Nature Center. "Once they reach the water, each female lays about 100 eggs, which stick to submerged branches."

Slitherton said that "one or two months later, the larvae begin to hatch. They are only half an inch (13 mm) long!" When they are about 5 months old, the babies metamorphose into tiny 2.5 inch (64 mm) adults, crawl out of the pond, and then back into the forest.

what spotted
salamanders eat:
-earthworms
-snails
-slugs
-spiders
-insects

AMAZING SALAMANDER FACT:
Adults may live as long as 20 or 30 years

## AMERICAN BULLFROG
*(Rana catesbeina)*

LENGTH: 3.5-8" (9-20.3 cm)
HABITAT: permanent freshwater ponds and lake edges

So you know how bears hibernate? Bullfrogs do too! Only they hole up in the mud below the ponds. When it finally gets warm again, the bullfrogs crawl out of the mud and warm themselves in the spring sunshine. They cannot move very fast until they warm up, though. I found out that bullfrog tadpoles can take up to two years to turn into adult frogs.

## GREAT BLUE HERON
*(Ardea herodias)*

HEIGHT: 39-52" (99-132 cm)  WINGSPAN: 70" (1.8 m)
HABITAT: lakes, ponds, rivers, and marshes

## Heron Hour: An Interview

*Planet Scout Gazette sent crack reporter Gretchen Askers to interview Dr. Bill Hunter, a member of the Sharpes Institute of Bird Beaks. Here's what she discovered:*

**How do we know what a heron eats?**
You can tell exactly what any bird eats by looking at its bill. A heron's beak is long and pointed. Beaks shaped like this are excellent for catching fish, frogs, voles, small turtles, and insects.

**How would a heron catch all those quick animals? Isn't it too big to sneak around?**
Herons hunt at the edges of ponds, where they wade quietly through the water, looking for food. They are careful not to make sudden movements.

**But wouldn't the heron cast a shadow over the water and scare the animals away?**
The light color of a heron's underside helps him fool his prey by blending in with the color of the sky as the frog or fish looks up.

RIO GRANDE LEOPARD FROG — rana berlandieri

CANADIAN TOAD — bufo hemiophrys

CARPENTER FROG — rana virgatipes

WOOD FROG — rana sylvatica

SOUTHERN CRICKET FROG — acris gryllus

NORTHERN LEOPARD FROG — rana pipiens

rana clamitans

NORTHERN CRICKET FROG — acris crepitans

GREEN FROG

SNOWY EGRET
egretta thula

LEAST BITTERN

ixobrychus exilis

AMERICAN BITTERN
botarus lentiginosus

WHITE-FACED IBIS

plegadis chihi

April 15
Hooray, I saw Mr. Green at the pond today! I missed my frog friend during the winter. He is an especially bulgy Bullfrog who I named for our bus driver— they are both kind of bulgy! What was he doing all winter? I'll have to find out. While I was watching Mr. Green from behind some common cattails, a Great Blue Heron landed in the pond. It was much bigger than I expected almost as tall as I am! I had never seen one so close before. It had a long, slinky neck like a snake, a thin, sharp beak like a sword, and tall, skinny legs like broom handles. What a lanky bird! It started to move closer and closer to Mr. Green. Oh no, I thought, is the heron going to try to eat my favorite frog? I jumped out from my hiding place to save him. Boy, was Mr. Heron surprised! Sorry, he'll have to find his lunch at another pond.

LITTLE BLUE HERON
egretta caerulea

YELLOW-CROWNED NIGHT-HERON

nycticorax violaceus

butorides striatus

BLACK-CROWNED NIGHT-HERON

nycticorax nycticorax

GREEN-BACKED HERON

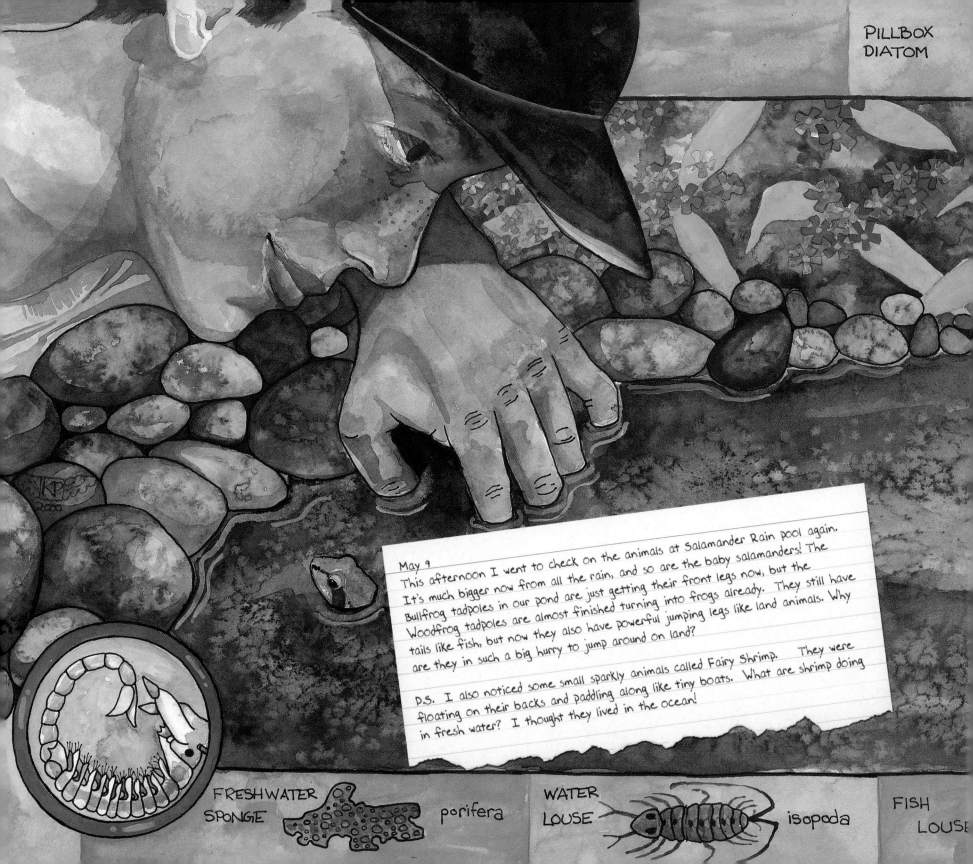

PILLBOX
DIATOM

**May 9**
This afternoon I went to check on the animals at Salamander Rain pool again.
It's much bigger now from all the rain, and so are the baby salamanders! The
Bullfrog tadpoles in our pond are just getting their front legs now, but the
Woodfrog tadpoles are almost finished turning into frogs already. They still have
tails like fish, but now they also have powerful jumping legs like land animals. Why
are they in such a big hurry to jump around on land?

P.S. I also noticed some small sparkly animals called Fairy Shrimp. They were
floating on their backs and paddling along like tiny boats. What are shrimp doing
in fresh water? I thought they lived in the ocean!

FRESHWATER
SPONGE                    porifera

WATER
LOUSE                     isopoda

FISH
LOUSE

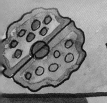

protista

FINGERNAIL CLAM

pisidiidae

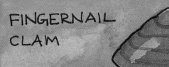

COPEPOD

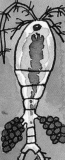

copepoda

HYDRA

hydrozoa

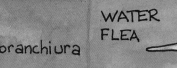

branchiura

WATER FLEA

cladocera

from Wetland Watchers Magazine

## WOOD FROG

*(Rana sylvavtica)*

LENGTH: 1.38-3.2"
(9-20.3 cm)

HABITAT: vernal pools

### Living frog-sicles

What does a cold-blooded amphibian do when it's cold enough to freeze a pond solid? If you're a toad, you might hibernate in underground rock chambers near streams. That's because running water keeps the temperature just above freezing.

But if you're a wood frog, gray tree frog, spring peeper, or chorus frog, you can just freeze solid and wait for spring.

The wood frog (*Rana sylvatica*) turns into one of these remarkable "frog-sicles." Wood frogs live in damp woodlands in the Southeastern United States (down to northern Georgia), and in Alaska and parts of Canada. The largest wood frogs are about 3-1/4 inches long. Their croak sounds like a small duck. Most have a dark facial mask, but their coloring ranges from yellowish-brown to pink, brownish-black, and black.

Bob Hay works for Wisconsin's Department of Natural Resources in Madison. He explains how the freezing process works. First, the frogs bury themselves in leaf litter. "When their [body] temperature reaches 32 to 33 degrees F, the body cells become saturated with a glycol-like substance," he says. This substance is equivalent to nature's antifreeze. It keeps the frog's cells from being damaged by freezing.

Scientists have discovered that up to 65 percent of the water in a wood frog's body can freeze. The water

# Small Survivors:

There are about 25 species of Fairy Shrimp. All depend upon vernal pools for survival. They spend their entire lives there to escape from being eaten by fish. Fairy Shrimp lay eggs that are able to withstand drying. The eggs hatch at the next flooding. Some eggs have hatched after waiting 20 years for the right conditions to return.

## FAIRY SHRIMP

*(Branchinecta paludosa)*

SIZE: usually no longer than 1" (2.5 cm)

HABITAT: vernal pools

THE CHRISTIAN SCIENCE MONITOR

**Pamela D. Jacobsen**

Tuesday, June 20, 2000

32°F.

freezes outside each cell, but not inside it. Ice crystals inside would cause damage.

After the antifreeze process is complete, the frog's heart stops beating and it stops breathing. All muscle movement halts. The frog appears to be frozen solid.

When spring arrives, the frogs thaw. How the heart starts beating and the lungs start breathing again is still a mystery.

ILLUSTRATIONS BY DAVE HERRING

# FISHING SPIDER
## (Dolomedes triton)
LENGTH: .4-.7" (1-1.8 cm)
HABITAT: rocks and plant stems near pond edges, also water surface

*I saw one of these spiders in our pond today. It kept on quickly jumping from one water plant to another.*

# POND CRAYFISH
## (Procambarus clarki)
LENGTH: 4-5" (10 – 12.5 cm)
HABITAT: ponds and streams

## Landlocked Lobsters

by Anne Tenna

Pond Crayfish are relatives of marine crabs, lobsters and shrimp. Like lobsters, they have 10 walking legs, the first pair of which is modified into a powerful set of pincers. Crayfish use these pincers to hold and tear their food, which consists mainly of plants. Crayfish are nocturnal, hiding under submerged rocks during the day. During dry seasons, they burrow into wet soil at the bottom of the pond.

*Did you know there are more than 200 different species of crayfish in North America?*

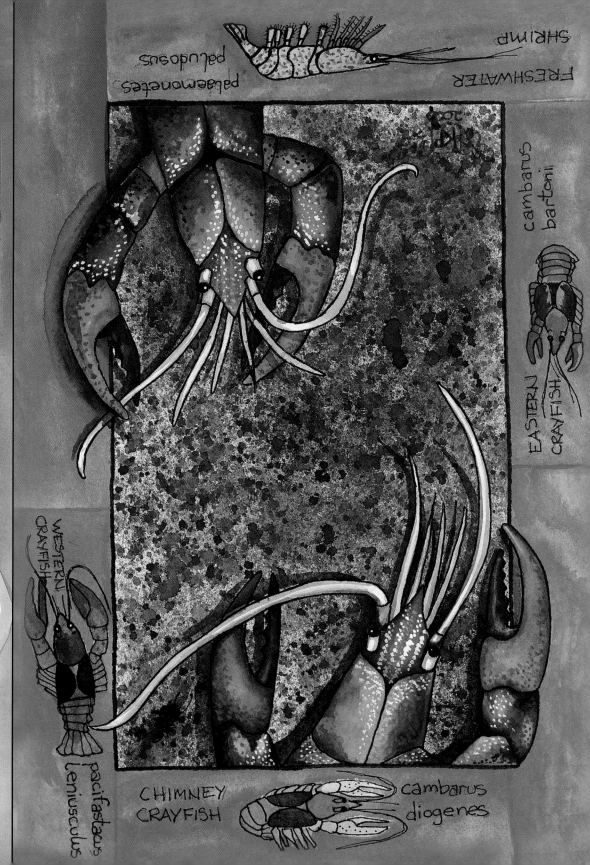

FRESHWATER SHRIMP
palaemonetes paludosus

EASTERN CRAYFISH
cambarus bartonii

WESTERN CRAYFISH
pacifastacus leniusculus

CHIMNEY CRAYFISH
cambarus diogenes

STREAK-WINGED RED SKIMMER

Sympetrum illotum

SUBARCTIC HAWKER

aeshna subarctica

TWELVE-SPOT SKIMMER

DARK LESTES

Lestes congener

BROWN DARNER

boyeria vinosa

WIDOW

Libellula luctuosa

July 4

Now we are visiting Grandma. She has a place right on Spider Lake, which is huge compared to our pond. The woods around her house go down to a tiny beach where she keeps a canoe. Kori and I have lots of time to explore. Today we were sitting on a log when I heard a buzz near my ear. A loose formation of blue and red bug rockets flew past. Dragon Flies and Damsel Flies! They looked as sleek and fast as Air Force fighter jets. I wonder why the rocket shape, and if they are predators. A Dragon Fly landed on my finger and we looked into each other's eyes. His were brown, like mine. I'm glad he didn't sting!

libellula
pulchella

SWIFT
LONG-
WINGED
SKIMMER

pachydiplax
longipennis

anax junius

GREEN DARNER

nannothemis
bella

BLUEBELL

# ELISA SKIMMER
## (Celithemis elisa)

A kind of dragonfly

SIZE: 1.125-1.375" (29-35 mm)
WINGSPAN: 2.25-2.375" (56-60 mm)
HABITAT: shallow bays, streams, and ponds

Did you know that dragonflies existed even before dinosaurs? It's true. They were as big as a model plane, with a wingspan of two feet!

21.

This insect's bright red abdomen makes it easy to spot in its green environment. Adults are active from April to October, when they mate and lay eggs. The nymphs spend the fall and winter in the water before emerging the following spring as adults.

# DAMSEL FLY
## (Argia spp.)

LENGTH: 11/8- 13/4" (29-43 mm)
   males slightly larger
HABITAT: gently flowing streams and lakes

# Powerful Predators:

Both damselflies and dragonflies are masters of air-to-air combat. Adults can fly in all directions with their four maneuverable wings. They can even hover in mid-air like helicopters. To catch prey, damselflies and dragonflies hook their bristly legs together, forming a bug-trapping basket.

Water Lilies, or lily pads, grow in quiet, muddy-bottomed ponds. I guessed their flat floating green leaves were about a foot (30 cm) wide. After I tipped over the canoe, I swam around in the lake and noticed that Water Lily stems extend down to the bottom of the lake, where the roots are anchored in the mud. Each pad is a separate plant, and produces a single white or pink flower with a yellow center. They smell good too!

## FRAGRANT WATER LILY

### (*Nymphaea odorata*)

BLOOMS: white or pink 3-5" (7.5-12.5 cm)
LEAVES: 4-12" (10-30 cm) diameter
HABITAT: ponds and quiet waters

## WATER LILY LEAF BEETLE

### (*Donacia spp.*)

SIZE: .25-.5" (6-12 mm)
HABITAT: water lilies

15. The Water Lily Leaf Beetle is a slender bronze insect with a green or yellow gloss to its shell. It lives on floating plants like the Fragrant Water Lily. The female cuts a tiny hole through the lily pad, and then cements the eggs to the underwater surface of the leaves. When the larvae hatch, they spin a shelter where they live for ten months before emerging as adults.

## SMALL DUCKWEED

### (*Lemma minor*)

HEIGHT: level with water surface
HABITAT: ponds & quiet water

Duckweed is one of the smallest and simplest flowering plants. It floats on the water surface, looking like handfuls of green confetti flung onto the pond. Unlike Water Lilies, Duckweed roots do not reach all the way to the pond bottom. Ducks and geese find it especially tasty.

WATER LETTUCE

pistia stratiotes

GOLDTHREAD

WATER SMART-WEED

polygonum amphibium

2000

coptis groenlandica

GOLDEN CLUB

orontium aquaticum

YELLOW POND LILY

nuphar variegatum

AMERICAN LOTUS

nelumbo lutea

YELLOW WATER LILY

nymphaea mexicana

July 10

This afternoon, Kori and I adventured around the lake in Grandma's canoe, which she lets us use as long as we promise always to wear life jackets. We steered through some green soup called Duckweed, and past a floating garden of white and yellow Water Lilies. I wanted to smell one, but I guess I reached a little too far. The canoe flipped over, and we landed in the water with two big splashes! At first Kori was mad, but she soon laughed and said, "Put both of us on your list of lake species!" Anyway, I got plenty of chances to smell the lilies and discovered that they have a nice fragrance. Lake mud doesn't smell so great, though.

RSH .IGOLD

caltha leptosepala

FLOATING HEARTS

nymphoides aquatica

GREEN SUNFISH
*lepomis cyanellus*

SAILFIN MOLLY
*poecilia latipinna*

*lepomis gulosus*
WARMOUTH

*micropterus punctulus*
SPOTTED BASS

GIZZARD SHAD

*dorosoma cepedianum*

LONGEAR SUNFISH
*lepomis megalotis*

BLACK CRAPPIE
*pomoxis nigromaculatus*

BLUEGILL
*lepomis macrohirus*

YELLOW PERCH
*perca flavescens*

JULY 30

This morning I was bird watching with my new binoculars, when I spotted a girl on the dock next door. I went over to see what she was looking at. Her name is Luna, and she was lying on her dock watching a school of Pumpkin Seed Fish swim around in the lake weed. She said I was smart because I knew their name. I showed her how to use my bird guide to identify the bird squawking and rattling in a tree above us. It was a Belted Kingfisher. Just then it shot down into the water, and surfaced with a minnow in its beak. Luna was really impressed and wants to be a Planet Scout!

LAUGHING KOOKABURRA
dacelo gigas
AFRICAN MANGROVE KING-FISHER
ceyx pictus

GREEN KINGFISHER
chlorocéryle americana
PUGNOSE MINNOW
notropis emiliae

PIED KINGFISHER
céryle rudis
AMAZON KINGFISHER
chlorocéryle amazona

BLUE-BREASTED KINGFISHER
halcyon malimbica
RINGED KINGFISHER
céryle torquata

# PUMPKIN SEED
## (Lepomis gibbosus)

LENGTH: to 10" (25 cm)
HABITAT: cool, quiet, shallow waters of slow streams, ponds, and lakes with dense vegetation

## Some Summer Sunfish

by R. E. Porter

If you are out by a northern lake this summer, look for the precocious Pumpkin Seed. (No, not the salty Halloween snack!) The Pumpkin Seed is a large type of sunfish that got its name from its orange seed-like spots. This fish is mostly a bottom feeder, eating snails, water insects, leeches, and small minnows. Interestingly, the male builds and guards the nest. Scout Leader Melvin Waterpepper says "this is a great fish to catch if you are a beginning fisher. It is very aggressive, and will go for almost any bait".

# BELTED KINGFISHER
## (Ceryle alcyon)

LENGTH: 13" (33 cm)
HABITAT: rivers, lakes, and saltwater estuaries

Luna and I read about the Belted Kingfisher after we identified it. Like herons, this bird has a sharp fishing bill. The Kingfisher hunts by plunging down from high branches to catch small fish underwater. Adult Kingfishers teach their young to fish by dropping dead meals into the water for them to retrieve. We learned the way to tell the males and females apart: the females have a rust-colored band across their white chests. We saw a female.

Joe Pye weed

# BEAVER
### (Castor canadensis)
LENGTH: 35.5-46" (90-117 cm)
HABITAT: streams and rivers, which they dam to create beaver ponds

## Beaver Trivia:

**Q:** How fast can a beaver build a dam?

**A:** A pair of beavers can build a two foot high, 12 foot long dam in two nights. Beavers build their dams so well that deer and other forest animals use them as bridges. They are motivated to fix their dams by the sound of running water.

from the Planet Scout Gazette

# Movers of the Earth

Beavers are not just cute, bucktoothed icons. They do major ecosystem engineering—from clear-cutting forests to filtering water.

BY DAVID LUKAS

March-April 2000 AUDUBON

**The Nature of Beaver Dams**

A beaver's ability to change the landscape is second only to that of humans. Since beavers prefer to dam streams in shallow, wooded valleys, the flooded area becomes wetlands and lush meadow, which sponge up floods and filter water. The inundated trees die, which provides habitat for a variety of cavity-nesting birds. Beavers use the water as protection from predators. With their webbed hind feet and paddlelike tails, they are efficient swimmers and can stay underwater for up to 15 minutes.

Inside a beaver lodge →

NUTRIA

myocastor coypus

ROUND-TAILED MUSKRAT

neofiber alleni

MINK

mustela vison

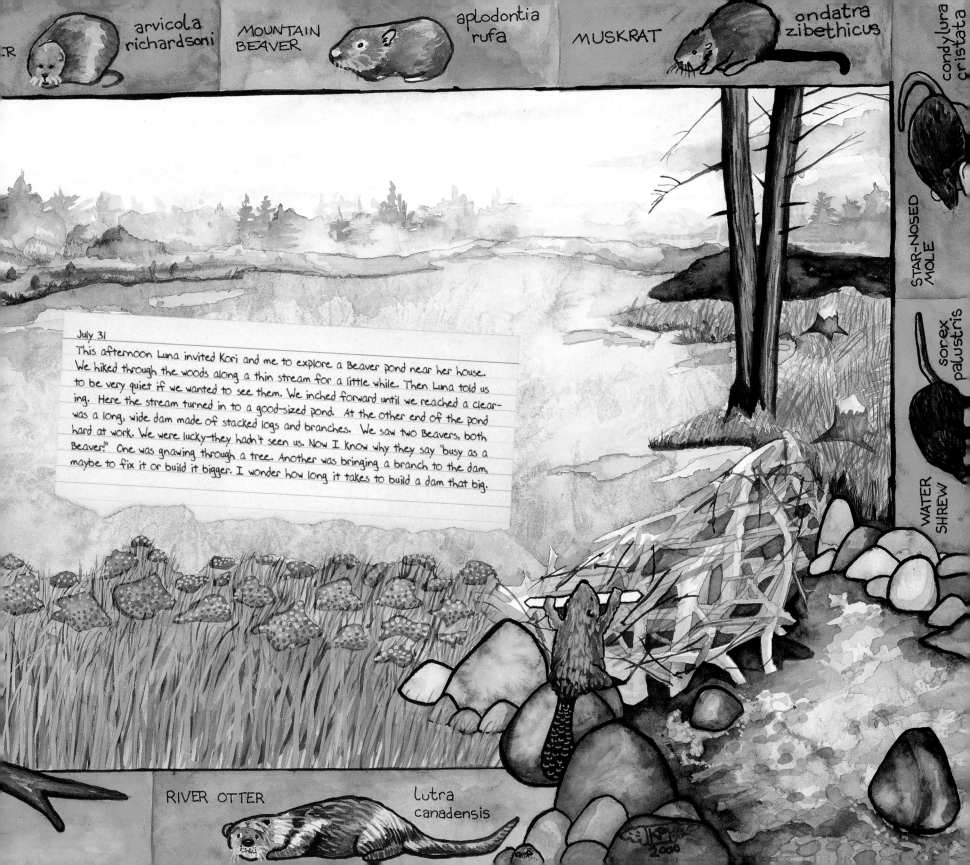

arvicola richardsoni

MOUNTAIN BEAVER

aplodontia rufa

MUSKRAT

ondatra zibethicus

condylura cristata

STAR-NOSED MOLE

sorex palustris

WATER SHREW

July 31

This afternoon Luna invited Kori and me to explore a Beaver pond near her house. We hiked through the woods along a thin stream for a little while. Then Luna told us to be very quiet if we wanted to see them. We inched forward until we reached a clearing. Here the stream turned in to a good-sized pond. At the other end of the pond was a long, wide dam made of stacked logs and branches. We saw two Beavers, both hard at work. We were lucky-they hadn't seen us. Now I know why they say "busy as a Beaver!" One was gnawing through a tree. Another was bringing a branch to the dam, maybe to fix it or build it bigger. I wonder how long it takes to build a dam that big.

RIVER OTTER

lutra canadensis

BARROW'S GOLDENEYE

bucephala islandica

ARCTIC LOON

gavia arctica

HOODED MERGANSER

lophodytes cucullatus

HORNED GREBE

podiceps auritus

WESTERN GREBE

aechmophorus occidentalis

EARED GREBE

podiceps nigricollis

PIED-BILLED GREBE

podilymbus podiceps

August 2

Kori and I got up early to watch Loons at the Brown Bridge Quiet Area. We just barely avoided a stinky incident with a mother skunk as she crossed our path leading her babies down to the shore. The best time to see Loons is at sunrise or at sunset, but when we got to the lake, it was foggy. We could sure hear them making their strange cries, though they sounded like they were very sad and lonely. Finally the mist cleared and we could see them. I noticed that Loons ride low in the water, much lower than ducks. Why is that? On the way back to Grandma's house, we saw a Zebra Swallowtail resting on a rock close by. Three black and white animals in the same day!

HESSEL'S HAIRSTREAK — mitoura hesseli

clossiana frigga — FRIGGA'S FRITILLARY

LEAST SKIPPERLING — ancyloxypha numitor

feniseca tarquinius

basicarchia archippus — HARVESTER

poanes massasoit — MULBERRY WING

VICEROY

PINK-EDGED SULPHUR — colias interior

# COMMON LOON
### (Gavia immer)
SIZE: 28–36" (71–91 cm)    DIVING DEPTH: to 200'
HABITAT: forested lakes; oceans and bays in winter

## Crazy as a Loon:

The Common Loon is one of three species of loons found in North America. Most other birds have hollow bones to help them float or fly. But loons' bones are solid, causing them to ride very low in the water, and helping them to dive deep like submarines. Loons have eerie calls that sound more like howling wolves than water birds. The echoes of the chilling calls make the northern lakes seem larger and lonelier.

### STRIPED SKUNK
### (Mephitis mephitis)
SIZE: to 2' (60 cm)
HABITAT: woods & pond edges

## Stinky Surprise!
*by R. E. Porter*

"When you are thinking about what animals you might see near a lake or a pond, you probably wouldn't think of a skunk," says Pepé Smelard, chairman of the Northwoods Skunk Study. "You might be surprised to learn that skunks often live at the edge of ponds, where they hunt duck and turtle eggs. If the eggs are too large," he laughed, "they launch them back through their legs at something hard to crack them open. But seriously," he said, "they also eat berries, insects, vegetables, mice and voles."

### ZEBRA SWALLOWTAIL
### (Eurytides marcellus)
SIZE: 2.4–3.5" (60–89 mm)
HABITAT: waterside woods, lakeshores

7

The Zebra Swallowtail is the most common of the North American Kite swallowtails. The Zebra Swallowtail is named for its bold black stripes. As caterpillars, Zebra Swallowtails also have stripes, but these are yellow and black.

# LAKE TROUT
### (Salvelinus namaycush)

LENGTH: to 4'2" (1.3 m)
HABITAT: deep cold waters of lakes in far north

WEIGHT: can weigh up to 125 lbs

## Scouting Trout
by Gretchen Askers

Lake Trout are the largest trout native to North America. They inhabit the deep, cold waters of northern lakes and rivers. Once revered by the Native Americans of the Great Lakes, the Lake Trout suffered from water pollution in the mid 20th century. Their populations in the Great Lakes were also severely depleted by an influx of parasitic Sea Lampreys caused by the building of a new canal between Lake Erie and the St. Lawrence Seaway in the 1940's.

# MALLARD
### (Anas platyrhnchos)

LENGTH: 18-27" (46-68 cm)
HABITAT: ponds, lakes, and marshes

## This End Up
by Gretchen Askers

Mallard Ducks belong to a group of ducks called "dabblers". Unlike Common Loons, which are divers, mallards feed in shallow water by tipping over to reach submerged pond plants. All you see is their toes and tails while the ducks are dabbling. Mallards make their nests of reeds and grasses, lining them with soft down. The nests are usually located near pond edges. The female builds the nest while the male defends the aquatic feeding area nearby. She usually lays 8-10 pale greenish white eggs. Did you know that domestic white farm ducks were originally bred from mallards?

CINNAMON TEAL — anas cyanoptera

BLUE WINGED TEAL — anas discors

DUCK POTATO

WHITE-CHEEKED PINTAIL — anas bahamensis

NORTHERN PINTAIL — anas acuta

sagittaria latifolia

AMERICAN WIGEON — anas americana

BAIKAL TEAL — anas formosa

NORTHERN SHOVELER — anas clypeata

CUTTHROAT TROUT

SOCKEYE SALMON

oncorhynchus nerka

BROWN TROUT

salmo trutta

MAYFLY ephem- eroptera

salmo clarki

ATLANTIC SALMON

salmo salar

salvelinus fontinalis

BROOK TROUT

RAINBOW TROUT

salmo gairdneri

APACHE TROUT

salmo apache

August 5
I sat on the dock swinging my legs over the edge and eating my sandwich. I was wondering how the tadpoles were doing back in our pond, when Luna showed up. She hadn't eaten lunch yet, so I gave her some of my sandwich. We spotted a family of paddling Mallard Ducks eating Duck Potatoes near the shore, so we threw them our bread crusts. We wondered where their nest might be. While we were enjoying the warm sun, we also saw a giant Lake Trout leaping out of the water after some tasty bugs. It must have been at least three feet long. Luna said that their species name, namaycush, means "denizens of the deep" in the Cree language. (She is part Cree herself, she said.) I wonder how deep Lake Trout really go.

SLIDER    pseudemys scripta    FLORIDA REDBELLY TURTLE    chrysemys nelsoni    CHIAPAS CROSS - BREASTED TURTLE    staurotypus salvinii

MANAMATA

chelus fimbriatus

SPINY SOFTSHELL

MAP TURTLE

graphtemys graphica

trionyx spiniferus

September 13
Well, I am back in school now. Our tiny backyard pond looked very different when we got home. The Bullfrog tadpoles are mostly grown up, but they still have small tails, and they are not as big as the adult Bullfrogs yet.
    I saw a pile of Painted Turtles basking in the afternoon sunshine. I wonder if they were trying to keep warm by sitting on each other in the cool autumn weather.

P.S. One of the turtles on the top had spots all over it. What kind of turtle was that?

SNAPPING TURTLE    chelydra serpentina    STINKPOT    sternotherus odoratus    WESTERN POND TURTLE    clemmys marmorata

PAWPAW

EASTERN
COTTONWOOD

asimina
triloba

populus
deltoides

HONEY
LOCUST

WATER
OAK

quercus
nigra

gleditsia
triacanthos

BLACK
WILLOW

salix
nigra

SYCAMORE

platanus
occidentalis

## PAINTED TURTLE
### (Chrysemys picta)

LENGTH: 4-9.875" (10.2-25.1 cm)  EGGS: 2-20
INCUBATION AVERAGE: 10-11 weeks
HABITAT: slow-moving streams, rivers and lakes

## Turtle Times
*by Gretchen Askers*

Looking for Turtles? Spring and fall are the best times to spot them out in the open. Like other reptiles such as snakes and lizards, turtles are cold-blooded. This means that they cannot generate their own body heat. Their bodies are always the same temperature as the air around them. In cooler months (when they are not hibernating), turtles and other reptiles search out sunny locations where they can rest and get warm. "This behavior is called basking," explains Dr. Norm Carapace, head of the North American Turtle Research Authority. "Painted Turtles, which are the most common turtles in North America, are very fond of basking. In fact, you can often spot dozens of them on the same log. Spotted Turtles are less common, sticking mostly to beaver ponds and vernal pools. They frequently keep company with Bog, Wood, and Painted Turtles."

## SPOTTED TURTLE
### (Clemmys guttata)

LENGTH: 3-5" (8-12.7 cm)  EGGS: 3-8
INCUBATION AVERAGE: 10-14 weeks,
HABITAT: wet woods, beaver ponds,
vernal pools

Did you know that you can tell if a spotted Turtle is a boy or a girl by looking at its eye color? It's true! Males have brown eyes and females have orange eyes.

# NORTHERN WATER SNAKE

*(Nerodia sipedon)*

SIZE: 22 - 53"
(55.9 - 134.6 cm)
HABITAT: woodlands and pond edges

I saw some baby snakes with their mother today. I looked them up in my reference book and found out that they are Northern Water snakes and that they aren't poisonous.

# How to Clean Up a Pond:

1. Get permission from the pond owner.
2. Remove any litter or garbage.
3. Determine if the pond is clogged with algae or other plants. If so, introduce locally native plant eaters such as ducks or tadpoles.
4. Make sure some of the pond's shoreline has appropriate vegetation coverage (mown grass all the way to the edge of the pond gives animals like frogs or birds no place to hide).
5. Build nesting boxes to attract birds.
6. Make sure the pond is deep enough to hold water all year.
7. Create a place where people can sit and enjoy the wildlife.

Melvin gave us this worksheet. Go to www.planetscouts.org if you want to learn more about restoring and cleaning up wetlands.

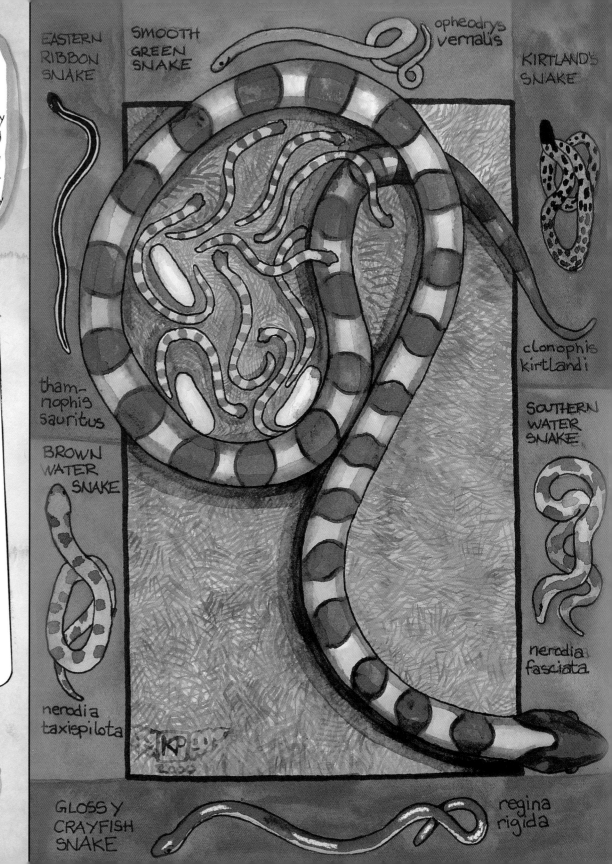

EASTERN RIBBON SNAKE

SMOOTH GREEN SNAKE

opheodrys vernalis

KIRTLAND'S SNAKE

clonophis kirtlandi

SOUTHERN WATER SNAKE

thamnophis sauritus

BROWN WATER SNAKE

nerodia fasciata

nerodia taxiespilota

GLOSSY CRAYFISH SNAKE

regina rigida

KLINT  lakes & ponds

STEPHANIE  rivers & streams

NICO  marshes & swamps

PHONG  bogs & fens

MELVIN  wetland patrol leader

ERIC  rivers & streams

KORI  lakes & ponds

School Pond

October 8

Today is Saturday. Kori and I invited the rest of the Wetland Patrol to our house for our monthly meeting. Kori showed everybody around the pond. We got a rare glimpse of some newborn Northern Water Snakes. These snakes hatch in the fall, so they were probably only a couple of weeks old. I told them about the different animals and plants we had seen at Spider Lake. For our annual service project, Melvin Waterpepper, leader of the Wetland Patrol, suggested that we all help clean up the pond near school. Everybody thought it would be a great idea. Then more kids could have fun pond adventures, and the clean pond would attract wetland creatures looking for a home.

ALEX bogs & fens

CINNAMON marshes & swamps

NORTHERN HARRIER
circus cyaneus

SWALLOW-TAILED KITE
elanoides forficatus

buteogallus anthracinus

COMMON BLACK-HAWK

buteo brachyurus

SHORT-TAILED HAWK

OSPREY
pandion haliaetus

SNAIL KITE
rostrhamus sociabilis

January 1

I decided to spend a little time at our pond today. It's all frozen over now—so quiet, so cold, so different. I was sitting on a frozen log, drinking a thermos of hot chocolate and wondering about Mr. Green sleeping somewhere down under the ice when I saw a Bald Eagle soaring high in the sky. It was not flapping its wings at all. I wonder if Bald Eagles migrate like songbirds, or brave the cold and storms of winter.

P.S. A special day! I got an email from from my cousin Kristin—she saw eagles, and also a postcard from Luna—she saw a moose!

BOBCAT   felis rufus

MOOSE

WHITE
TAILED
DEER

odcoileus
virginianus

BLACK
BEAR

ursus
americanus

# MOOSE
## (Alces alces)

SIZE: 6.75-9' long (206-279 cm) 6' (180 cm) high at the withers

MALE ANTLERS: 4-5' (120-150 cm) wide, palmate

HABITAT: swamps, aspen and willow thickets, ponds

Dear Klint,     December 30

Happy New Year! I just joined the Planet Scouts this fall. Today when I was doing some exploring in the woods I saw a huge moose that was as big as a truck. It had HUGE antlers and made funny moose noises.

See you next summer up at the lake.

USA 32

Klint V.
c/o Wetland
Patrol No. 1
Metamora, MI

From: Kristin
To: Klint V.
Subject: Bald Eagle Sightings

Dear Klint-
Happy New Year!
Today I drove up the
River Road from St.
Louis to do some
eagle watching.
There were loads of
people out today,
even though it was
freezing cold. They
all stood on the side

# BALD EAGLE
## (Haliaeetus leucocephalus)

LENGTH: 30-31" (76-79 cm)

EGGS: 1-3 bluish white

HABITAT: coasts, lakes, rivers in open and forests

of the road with binoculars glued to their faces.
The eagles spend the winter here because the
Mississippi River rarely freezes over this far
south, and there are lots of fish to eat here. I
stayed outside for about half an hour and count-
ed 14 Bald Eagles. They were so graceful diving
and swooping over the river. I am glad they are
coming back, after being on the endangered
species list for so long!

Love, Kristin

# So what CAN I do?

## 1. Read a book!

**Swampwalker's Journal: A Wetlands Year**
by David Carroll
Houghton Mifflin Co., Boston © 1999

**Around the Pond**
by Ann Cooper illustrated by Dorothy Emerling
Denver Museum of Natural History Press © 1998

**The Great Lakes**
by Sharon Katz
Benchmark Books, New York © 1999

**National Audubon Society Nature Guides: Wetlands**
by William Neiring
Alfred A. Knopf, New York © 1998

**Back Yard Bugs**
by Robin Kittrel Laughlin
Chronicle Books, San Franscisco © 1996

## 2. Get on the Web!

**The National Audubon Society**
www.audubon.org
**The National Wildlife Federation**
www.nwf.org
**Acorn Naturalists**
www.acornnaturalists.com
**Great Lakes Aquarium**
www.glaquarium.org
**The Cousteau Society**
www.cousteau.org
**U.S. Fish and Wildlife Service**
www.savewetlands.org

## 3. Join the PLANET SCOUTS!

Join the Planet Scouts and participate in making a change today for the good of our planet!

Find out how you can help make a difference by logging on to www.planetscouts.org.

## MEET THE AUTHOR

DEAR PLANETSCOUTS—

Hi! My name is Kristin. I am the author and illustrator of this book. I live in St. Louis with my husband, our dog, and 2 cats. When I am not making books, I like to work in my garden and read books. I have always wanted to be an artist. In 9th grade I made my first children's book for a school project. After that, I decided to be an author too. This is my fourth book. I hope you like it!

kristin@planetscouts.org

I would like to thank the following people for their wonderful help in making this book possible:

## THANK YOU!

**GABRIEL SERAFINI**
my husband
**KATHY PRATT**
my mother
**KATIE PRATT**
my sister
**KEN PRATT**
my father
**KEVIN PRATT**
my brother
**KORI VIZENA**
my cousin

**MICHEAL BOOTH**
research assistant
**PRESTON LARIMER**
zoology professor
**GLENN HOVEMANN**
text editor
**MUFFY WEAVER**
art editor
**DAWN PUBLICATIONS
STAFF**

and especially
**KLINT VIZENA**
my cousin, for the use of his handwriting and his special pond in this story.

Printed in Hong Kong
10 9 8 7 6 5 4 3 2 1
First Edition
Design by Kristin Joy Pratt-Serafini
Additional design and computer production by Andrea Miles

**Library of Congress Cataloging-in-Publication Data**

Pratt, Kristin Joy.
   Salamander rain : a lake and pond journal / by Kristin Joy Pratt-Serafini.
    p. cm. — (A sharing nature with children book)
   Includes bibliographical references (p.   ).
   ISBN 1-58469-017-8 (pbk.) — ISBN 1-58469-018-6 (hardback)
   1. Wetland animals—Juvenile literature. [1. Wetland animals. 2. Wetland ecology. 3. Ecology.]  I. Title. II. Series.
   QL113.8 .P73 2001
   577.68—dc21

00-012066

**Salamander Rain** represents Kristin's long-awaited reappearance as an author and illustrator—and as an environmental educator in her own right.

As a 15 year old youngster she wrote and illustrated **A Walk in the Rainforest.** At age 17 she followed with the best-selling **A Swim through the Sea.** At 19 she did **A Fly in the Sky.**

Praise poured in. She was pronounced an "Eco-Star" by The Cousteau Society; Jacques Cousteau toasted Kristin as "an inspiration for all young environmentalists." The Children's Book Council of the National Science Teacher's Association declared **A Swim Through the Sea** an Outstanding Science Trade Book For Children For 1995.

Kristin took time out from book-making to pursue her studies, especially studio art. She graduated from college, married, and changed her last name to Pratt-Serafini. What we see now in Kristin is a self-assured writer and artist, very environmentally aware, whose work is still juicy and fun.

*A Note to Teachers:* to facilitate using picture books in the classroom, Dawn Publications offers Teacher's Guides for each of Kristin's books (and those of several other authors as well). These 48-page guides offer lesson plans for grades 3 to 6 that are distinctive in that they integrate core science and language arts curricula with character education lessons.

## Some Related Books from Dawn Publications

**Salmon Stream** by Carol Reed-Jones. By the author of *The Tree in the Ancient Forest*, this book is lively and rhythmic, rich in imagery, yet well founded in the scientific cycle of salmon. It engages children in a positive way, and shows how they can help make sure salmon will always be with us.

**The Tree in the Ancient Forest** by Carol Reed-Jones. A single old tree is home for owls and voles, squirrels and martens, and many other creatures of the deep woods. Through cumulative verse this book tells the tale of their community—a wonderful introduction to the interdependence of nature.

**My Favorite Tree**, by Diane Iverson. Each major family of indigenous North American trees is illustrated with a child engaged with it in some way, along with a map and a variety of information about its major features, its role in history, its wild animal companions, and other interesting facts.

**This Is the Sea that Feeds Us**, by Robert F. Baldwin. In simple cumulative verse, beginning with tiny plankton, "floating free," this book explores the oceans' fabulous food chain that reaches all the way to whales and humans in an intricate web.

**A Drop Around the World**, by Barbara McKinney. Follow a drop a water in its natural voyage around the world, in clouds, as ice and snow, underground, in the sea, piped from a reservoir, in plants and even in an animal. Science of the water cycle and poetic verse come together in this book. *Teacher's Guide available.*

Dawn Publications
P.O. Box 2010
Nevada City, CA 95959
800-545-7475
nature@dawnpub.com
www.dawnpub.com

Dawn Publications is dedicated to inspiring in children a deeper understanding and appreciation for all life on Earth. To order, or for a copy of our catalog, please call 800-545-7475. You may also order, view the catalog, see reviews and much more online at www.dawnpub.com.